MARIAH CAREY · M

M000159509

ISBN: 0-7935-2986-7

Hal Leonard Publishing Corporation

7777 West Bluemound Road P.O. Box 13819 Milwaukee, WI 53213

ALL I'VE EVER WANTED

Words and Music by MARIAH CAREY
and WALTER AFANASIEFF

ANYTIME YOU NEED A FRIEND

Words and Music by MARIAH CAREY
and WALTER AFANASIEFF

DREAMLOVER

Words and Music by MARIAH CAREY
and DAVE HALL

Do do do do do do do, ooh _____

ba - by. _____

I need a lov - er to give _____ me _____
I don't want an - oth - er pre - tend - er _____

HERO

Words and Music by MARIAH CAREY
and WALTER AFANASIEFF

I'LL NEVER FORGET YOU

Words and Music by MARIAH CAREY
and BABYFACE

I'VE BEEN THINKING ABOUT YOU

Words and Music by MARIAH CAREY,
DAVID COLE and ROBERT CLIVILLES

JUST TO HOLD YOU ONCE AGAIN

Words and Music by MARIAH CAREY
and WALTER AFANASIEFF

MUSIC BOX

Words and Music by MARIAH CAREY
and WALTER AFANASIEFF

NOW THAT I KNOW

Words and Music by MARIAH CAREY,
DAVID COLE and ROBERT CLIVILLES

WITHOUT YOU

Words and Music by WILLIAM HAM
and TOM EVANS

Slow rock

no chord

mp

legato

No, I

F(add9)

can't for-get ___ this eve-ning or your face as you were leav-ing, but I

Am(add9)

Gm(add9)

guess that's just the way the sto-ry goes.

A7sus   A7

You al-ways

Dm

smile but in your eyes ___ your sor-row shows.

Dm/C   Bm7♭5

Yes, it